Coyote for a Day

Coyote for a Day

Roger Caras

Illustrated by Diane Paterson

Windmill Books, Inc.
and
E. P. Dutton
New York

Text copyright © by Roger Caras 1977
Illustrations copyright © by Diane Paterson 1977
Published by Windmill Books & E. P. Dutton
201 Park Avenue South, New York, New York 10003

LIBRARY OF CONGRESS CATALOGING IN PUBLICATION DATA

Caras, Roger A
Coyote for a Day.
SUMMARY: Follows the activities of a coyote and
its mate as they forage for food and try to keep out
of danger.
1. Coyotes—Juvenile literature.   [1. Coyotes—
Habits and behavior]   I. Paterson, Diane, 1946–
II. Title.
QL795.C6C37   599'.74442   77-3895
ISBN: 0-525-61543-1

Published simultaneously in Canada by Clarke,
Irwin & Company, Limited, Toronto and Vancouver
Edited by Robert Kraus
Designed by Cary Rockwell
Printed in the U.S.A.   First Edition

10 9 8 7 6 5 4 3 2 1

For
Ch. the Rectory's Yankee Patriot,
Jeremy Boob and Peter's Peace

Today you are a coyote. That really means that you are a kind of wolf; Not the great timber wolf of northern forests, but the small brush wolf of open prairies and even farmlands.

That also means that you are one of the smartest animals in all the wild world of animals. You have to be smart just to stay alive.

The Indians who once lived on the great lands where you now live said that you invented man. They also said you were a magician and that you spoke with the beings who lived in the clouds. Well, the Indians are almost all gone now and so are the stories they told about you, the great bison herds (we sometimes call those animals buffalo, but they are really bison) on which the Indians lived have just about vanished, too. (A few do live on in parks and zoos but that isn't the same thing at all.) All that is left is you and at night you sing the saddest of songs, you roll your voice into the sky but the cloud beings no longer answer.

But this day is different, as the sun starts to fall away beyond the far edge of the world, you sit on a small, grass-covered hill and start your song, the one the Indians heard, and the people who crossed your land in covered wagons. The sun slips away at last to sleep on the other side of the world, and you are left with the great sky and the stars that begin blinking down at you. The darker it gets the lonelier your song seems to be and the brighter the stardust across the sky shines down.

In a secret place the cranky old badger hears your song and stops to listen. The prairie dogs in their burrows hear it, too, but they are underground and safe. The owl flying low over the land in search of its nighttime meal hears your song, but he doesn't have to worry for his talons are strong and his flight powerful. Smaller creatures hear you and they huddle close to the thickest grass and brush, for they know the little wolf who sings is also a hunter.

Then suddenly you stop, for you hear something. The night is answering you this time. You are not alone, and from another hill not far off, another night voice rolls up into the sky and across the wide open grasslands until it reaches your sensitive ears. You cock your head and listen and then you sing again, louder and more clearly, even, than before. Then you wait, but not for long, and the other song rolls again toward you in the night. For an hour you sing your duet. Sometimes you sing alone, one at a time, one answering the other, and sometimes you sing together, laying your songs on top of each other. All around you the world listens and the stars shine down and their silver light is like a shower of sparks that lingers on the tips of your thick fur.

Because you are a coyote you know things only the little wolf can know. It is not in the same way a man can know something —not with thoughts—but in a deeper way, down deep inside. And the thing you know now is that the time has come to end your song. On the other hill the coyote there knows, too, and the night is silent except for the faintest whisper of the wind. All around the other animals listen and wait, for they know something important has happened. It is always important when the night answers the night.

You know, in your coyote way, from the song you heard that the little wolf of the other hill, the one you have never seen is a female. She knows, too, that you are a male, and as your songs end you each slip like small gray ghosts down into the valley between the hills. Soon you are standing close to each other, whining softly, speaking the quiet talk of the little brush wolf. The little female coyote, for she is smaller than you are, bites you gently on the muzzle. It is soft, a touch, really, and it doesn't hurt at all. It is a signal, though, a sign that she now will remain with you and hunt by your side and sing with you in the night until your cubs are born. Then you will raise those cubs together as a family. She is now your mate.

After whining and nibbling gently on her muzzle as well, you move off together to find your meal. You move quietly through some deep grass and then you both, just as if a signal had been given, stop. You stand so perfectly still there is no sound and your brownish gray coats blend into the night. You are invisible. The signal that turned you both into statues was a small sound in the grass ahead of you. A hare, a jackrabbit, has been hiding there. It listens, hears nothing, and then moves. You and your mate explode into action. It is soon over and you share your meal. It is not cruel, for nature made you the hunter and the jackrabbit your prey. Besides, he had grown very old and no longer was fast and smart enough to stay alive in a world of hunters. If you and your mate had not eaten that night, the owl would have, or perhaps the rattlesnake.

The night passes and you and your mate still trot along side by side across the open prairie. As soon as the sun begins climbing into the sky from behind the hills to the east, long fingers of orange and yellow light begin creeping across the sky. It is then that you hear that sound. Again you freeze, for it is a sound of danger and you must find where it is coming from.

Bzzzzzzzzzzzzzzzzzzzzzz

Bzzzzzzzzzzzzzzzzzzzzzz

The angry sound of the rattlesnake's tail tells you that this other night hunter is nearby. It is crawling away to hide before the sun is really high. It is summer and the hot sun can kill a snake. It is looking for a place of deep shadows to wait for the day and the sun to pass before it hunts again.

Bzzzzzzzzzzzzzzzzzzzzzzzz
Bzzzzzzzzzzzzzzzzzzzzzzzz

Again the heavy snake with the arrow-shaped head signals his anger. Cautiously you and your mate move forward, for your paths have crossed that of the dangerous legless hunter and his bite carries poison enough to cripple, perhaps even to kill you. Then you see him. He has moved beneath a low bush and has his head resting on top of his coiled body. Behind his head his tail stands straight up and moves so fast it is only a blur.

Bzzzzzzzzzzzzzzzzzzzzzzzz
Bzzzzzzzzzzzzzzzzzzzzzzzz

He would be good to eat, but only a coyote sick with hunger would take a chance and hunt the rattlesnake. You and your mate move around the bush in a wide circle. Long after you have passed, the rattlesnake continues to vibrate his tail.

The bright morning sun has now climbed high into the sky and the grass glistens yellow and gold. During the night, millions of little spiders spun their webs from grass blade to grass blade to catch the night-flying insects, for the spiders, too, are hunters. And now these webs hold tiny drops of morning dew. Strung out like jewels on the fine silk web lines, they form a field of glistening diamonds through which you and your mate now move. Although each line in a spider web is much stronger than steel would be if it were as fine, even the paw of the little wolf can shatter the web. Drops of dew splatter on your fur and you and your mate sparkle, too, in the sun, as you move through the field of gems and broken mirrors.

Coyotes know more about their world each moment of each day than man does about his, for the coyote has more enemies and faces many more dangers. Suddenly you and your mate freeze. There has been no signal between you, but there has been something—a signal from beyond. It says DANGER— there is danger in your land.

Neither you nor your mate is sure if you have heard something or seen something—perhaps it has been a small trace on the soft morning breeze. Perhaps it is something you have smelled, somehow, though, somehow you know you must not move, you must be silent like the rock on the hillside, as silent as the cloud in the sky.

Slammmmmmmmmmmmmmm-Spurrrrrrrtttt

The explosion goes off between you. Sand and bits of rock shower against your sides, stinging bits of earth torn loose by a heavy lead bullet.

Slammmmmmmmmmmmmmm-Spurrrrrrrrtttt

It comes again near your mate's front feet.

But now you are running, and this is another thing that comes inside the coyote. It is a trick you both know in the coyote way. Without a signal between you, you run in opposite directions. You zigzag and vanish and the man on the small hill with the gun no longer has a target to shoot at. He lowers his gun and stares out on an empty land that has swallowed two coyotes. You have become shadows, but soon even they are lost and the man with the gun who wanted your fur understands some of the things the Indians once said of you and your ways.

An hour later and many miles away from the man and his gun, you begin again to search for your mate. You knew to seek thick grass and rocky places so that your feet would not leave marks. If the man had had trained dogs with him, he could have chosen and followed either of you, for there is no way for a coyote to hide his smell. But the hunter was alone and try as he would he could find no paw marks on hard rock, none in deep grass that was strong and young and sprang back into place as soon as you passed. You are safe, but you are alone again.

You wait until it is dark, wait for the time when the guns of men are blind. And you seek a hilltop and begin your song of loneliness. Almost at once the answer comes. On a hilltop near-by your mate has been waiting. When you ran from the exploding danger of the gun, you each moved in a great circle and can easily rejoin again—another coyote way, another trick born inside you that helps you survive. The song between you is brief and you move down into the shadowy place and soon are nibbling each other's muzzles and lips again in greeting.

You move carefully now, and when day comes, you stay in narrow places between hills and along the edges of rivers and streams, places where trees and bushes grow and where you can hide. Your mate makes a hungry sound and soon you know why. The smell of fresh meat is strong and you both move toward it. In the distance a small lamb lies dead and it would be good to eat. But as you move toward it you come upon a shiny blue-black crow, it is dead, and beyond that a magpie, white, black and blue, is also dead. Your coyote mind can not understand poison and you do not really know that men have placed small pinches of deadly white powder in the body of the lamb so that if you eat you will die. But you do understand danger and you whine at your mate. She obeys your signal and you move in a wide circle and walk again along a riverbank.

A mile beyond the dead lamb and the birds that had been killed by the powder that was meant for you as well, you again smell something placed in your way by man. It is a trap, a machine that can catch and hold your foot. Again your sharp coyote senses tell you there is something wrong and again you move in a wide circle around the place of danger.

At last you come to a great open land. It is far from your enemy, man, and his tricks and ways. Both you and your mate are hungry and you hunt together. You move toward deep, grassy places, rise up on your hind legs and with your thin front legs stiff, you prance on the grass. Mice, grasshoppers, toads and other good things to eat are startled by your dance and move. You and your mate quickly gobble up everything you see and soon your hunger is gone.

The day passes without further danger and you sit side by side on a hill and sing together. Your song rolls across the prairie and in a valley not too far off, a band of wild horses hears it and the mares flick their ears and tails and huddle together. On another hill the great male horse, the stallion, stands guard. Your song brings comfort to him, for it means man is not nearby and man is the enemy of the wild horse, too. Somehow, in his horse way, the stallion senses the safety in your song, he tosses his head and snorts, you hear that sound in the dark, but continue your song.

Deep down inside, your coyote senses tell you another great secret, your mate has cubs growing inside her. In only a few weeks she will need a safe and quiet place for them to be born. With the birth of the morning's sun, your search begins.

You search the stream banks, along the river and each valley you come upon as you move away from man.

And at last, after several days have passed, you come upon an old badger hole. The cranky old badger has moved away and you and your mate begin deepening and widening the hole. You bring mouthfuls of dry grass and leaves and carry them down. Soon, in the deepest place, a cozy nest is formed. Here your babies will first appear and drink their mother's rich, warm milk. When they are old enough, it will be from this deep nest that they will first venture forth and learn to hunt and to fear man. For in your own special way you understand that only the coyote who knows to fear man can survive to find a mate and have puppies to continue your kind, only because you fear man can you still fill the sky with your wild song of the night.